The Book Journey Mentor's™ Guide to Self-Publishing

Written by
Daniella Blechner

Conscious Dreams
PUBLISHING

The Book Journey Mentor's™ Guide to Self-Publishing

Written by Daniella Blechner.

Non-fiction: Publishing

Copyright © 2016 by Daniella Blechner

All rights reserved. This book or any portion thereof may not be reproduced, shared publicly or privately or used in any manner whatsoever without the express written permission of the publisher except for the use of brief quotations in a book review.

Printed in the United Kingdom

First Printing 2016.

Published by Conscious Dreams Publishing.

www.consciousdreamspublishing.com

Edited by Wendy and Anna Yorke

Typeset by Nadia Vitushynska

Cover Design by Jae Thompson

ISBN 978-1913674205

This book belongs to

....

Contents

Introduction 7
My Story 9

STEP 1: The Vision. 3 Essential Tips to Self-Publishing 13
   1. What Is Your Why? 14
   2. Surround Yourself with Positive People 20
   3. Create a Clear Vision 22

STEP 2: Ingramspark and ISBNs. Publishing and Distribution 31
   Traditional versus Self-Publishing 34
   Publishing and Distribution 36
   ISBNs 37

STEP 3: The Edit. To Cut or Not to Cut? That Is the Question! 41
   The Edit 42
   The Blurb 47

STEP 4: Typesetting. A Time to Typeset 49
   What is Typesetting? 50
   Layout 51

STEP 5: Book Cover. How to Create a 'Drop the Mic' Book Cover 57
   Forget What You Have Been Told! 58
   My Book Cover Story 59
   Deciding on Your Concept 60
   Top 10 Tips to a 'Drop the Mic' Book Cover 62

STEP 6: Promotion. 7 Ways to Promote Your Book 63
   7 Ways to Promote Your Book 66
   Your Book Launch 70
   Ultimate Goal 71

STEP 7: Press. How to Get Your Book in the Press 73
   Public Relations for Your Book 74
   Top 10 Tips for Approaching Press 75

BONUS MATERIAL: Securing Retailers 79
   Advanced Information Sheet 83
   Links to Stockists, Retailers and Suppliers 84

INTRODUCTION

Everybody has a story within. Our story does not define us but if we can learn and grow from it, we can use it to empower and be of great service to other people. You are on this journey because you have a story inside: you have something to teach; a message to give; and a life or 1 million lives you want to touch. Congratulations on taking that first step. This guide will take you through the 7 Steps of Publishing. Throughout, I want you to hold close to the following two questions.

"Who am I?" and "What is my story?"

Be clear about who you are, what message you want to convey and how you want to impact people, and you will attract that which seeks you.

But before I take you on this journey, here is some information about me...

The Book Journey Mentor™

Congratulations on taking the first step to self-publishing. Many people dream of becoming a published author, but few take action.

Before you read my story, I want you to consider the following questions. What motivated you to take that step? Who do you want to impact with your story? How will you create your legacy?

When I look at people I always wonder, what did you dream of when you were a child? Do you have forgotten dreams that deep in your heart you are still passionate about achieving?

When I was young, my teachers frequently asked me what I wanted to be when I grew up. I always had a clear sense of who I was and what I wanted to do when I was very young (although this got lost on the way to adulthood!). I always said I wanted to be a vet and as I lover of James Herriot, I also wanted to write and publish a book (after I was 40!). I always wrote in detail about how I wanted to impact people positively and help to make the world a better place.

Well, I didn't become a vet — I became a teacher and mentor working with young people. I did write and publish three books (UNDER 35!). I am the founder of **Conscious Dreams Publishing**. I coach, mentor and advise aspiring authors, assisting them along their book journey and self-publishing process ensuring that they, at the end of it all, have a high quality and professional book, which will literally live forever.

I urge you today to always stay true to your dream. Publishing a book was not easy. I faced many rejections from agents and publishers. I believe strongly though, that when you are determined, passionate and clear about your vision, purpose and *why*, nothing will stop you. I learnt that no one is an island. We cannot do it alone. When fear and doubt speak to you telling you, "You can't", tell them "I CAN AND I WILL!" You need to know it is important to surround yourself with people who support your vision and encourage your dreams. You need to know it is important to have continued faith in your vision. You need to know the road may be hard but so worth it in the end. YOUR dream is too important to shelve.

Congratulations on taking the first step!

MY STORY

I am a self-confessed Ex, I repeat, Ex Mr Wrong magnet. I had so many Mr Wrong scenarios and dating disaster stories that my friends kept telling me to write them down. A title flashed before me, *Mr Wrong*. That was it! It was to be a collection of real life relationship stories written by women across the world who had encountered these infamous Mr Wrong characters but also a place where we could share stories and self-discover rather than blame. I am a strong believer that if we keep on attracting the same sort of situation, circumstance and person into our lives there is a limiting belief system that needs to change inside. I started creating various Mr Wrong characters I had encountered and got my friend and talented animator, Amde Anbessa-Ebanks to draw the sketches for me. Soon after, another friend and talented animator, Jason Lee, jumped on board too.

*Mr Loose Eye
c/o Amde Anbessa-Ebanks*

*How to ask for what you want!
c/o Jason Lee*

I wanted to reach out to women and find out if others could identify with these characters, as well as women who had encountered similar scenarios. In 2012, I set up a blog and I simply put a call out on my Facebook account asking if anyone could help me. Within minutes, another dear friend Candy Ellie contacted me and invited me round and then very patiently taught me how to set up and navigate myself around the world of blogging.

The reason I mention the people who assisted me in the beginning stages, is to highlight to you the importance of being surrounded by people who support, assist and also believe in your vision. I am blessed to not only know so many talented people, but also people who are willing to assist me in my journey and want to see me succeed. I want you to think about the people in your closest circle. Do they add value to your life? Do they support your dreams? Do they believe in your vision?

Having set up the blog and added the character sketches and descriptions, I put out a call out to women. I wanted to hear from women who had Mr Wrong stories, dating disaster quips and stories of overcoming toxic relationships. Before I knew it, I was inundated with stories from women from all over the world, from Canada to the USA, to Australia and Britain.

Excited, I began to write the book. After writing the first three chapters, I contacted agents. I was rejected. After a round of agent hunting and waiting 3-5 months for replies, I contacted publishers. I was rejected. The emails or letters were friendly and most wished me every success on my journey. The agents seemed to be looking for authors with a larger following or clear marketing strategy and the publishers were not accepting manuscripts from unsolicited authors.

I was determined not to let rejection get the better of me. I believed so strongly in what I was doing and, more importantly, the impact I wanted to have. I wanted to unite, inspire and empower women through the sharing of our stories and provide a platform for us to self-discover. I believed in the impact I wanted to have so much, that in my heart and in my soul, I already saw the book as published. It was just figuring out the best route.

I looked into self-publishing and was inundated with offers to publish my book without having read it. Having worked so hard on my manuscript, I felt that where was something fundamentally wrong with that. Where was the integrity? I didn't just want to just 'be published'. I wanted to add value. I wanted my book to be treated with care and to earn its place in the world of publishing. Some of these companies charged thousands and thousands of pounds to get my book to print and deliver my dreams but it was then I realised there was so much I could do myself. I wanted to feel empowered.

I published *Mr Wrong* on 20th Sept 2014 through my own company, **Conscious Dreams Publishing**. On the day of publication, it hit three bestseller lists on Amazon and was placed above *The Joy of Sex* (Alex Comfort), *The Rules* (Ellen Fein and Sherrie Schneider) and yes, the infamous *Think Like a Man, Act Like a Lady* (Steve Harvey). There are no words to describe the feeling of seeing your first book in print, yet alone ranking above noted authors such as these. I felt empowered.

Now I want you to feel empowered too. If you read, make notes, use the workbook provided and utilise the tools and resources here, there is no reason you cannot do the same.

My role as your Book Journey Mentor™ is to assist you on this voyage through the self-publishing process and teach you all there is to know. I am dedicated to helping you realise your dream and your vision and create the professional and powerful book you deserve.

Enjoy the journey, for it truly is a journey and one certainly worth taking!

"Be the author of your own destiny."
Daniella ☺

STEP 1: THE VISION

3 Essential Tips to Self-Publishing

1. WHAT IS YOUR WHY?

Everyone has a story inside; a unique journey, and purpose. We all have our reasons for wanting to do things and a desire to fulfil goals and dreams in our lives. But what is our why? Simon Sinek[1], visionary and author of *Start with Why*, believes that success does not stem from what we do but why we are doing it.

Many of us go to work every day with no idea as to why and we end up feeling unfulfilled. When we know why we are doing it and are more than comfortable with the answer, we are in a much better position to connect, inspire and empower other people. What is your book's *raison d'etre*[2]?

Three important questions to consider before you read any further.

1. What is your **why**? (Key driving force behind why you are writing the book?)
2. What is the **message** you want to convey?
3. What **impact** do you want your book to have on the reader?

These three questions are key to aligning your book, your message and your *raison d'etre* — your purpose — with your valuable readers. If you are unsure, find a trusted friend or loved one and ask them to support you in getting to the root of your intentions behind your book.

Here is an example.

My reason for writing *Mr Wrong* was because I was passionate about giving women a platform to have their stories shared without judgement. I felt that through breaking taboos, we would become more honest about our own experiences.

My message is tied to my *why*. I felt that there were so many relationship books that tell us, as women, who to be, how to be, how to act, how to think and how to play games in order to land that perfect man or relationship but nothing that told us, how to discover our own inner power, establish our values, identify our own wants and needs. My message to women was to seek within for answers and learn from past choices and become empowered by them by learning to let go and forgive our pasts, identify, examine and challenge limiting belief systems and make more empowering choices.

---

1   *https://www.startwithwhy.com/about/biography*
2   *Reason for being (French)*

The impact I wanted to have was to change the hearts and minds of women by giving them this platform to share, laugh and cry — but above all — become empowered by realising that they have the power to create their own lives through the choices they make and belief systems they hold.

What is your **why**, **message** and **impact**?

1. What is your **why**? (Key driving force behind why you are writing the book?)

   ....
   ....
   ....
   ....
   ....
   ....

2. What is the **message** you want to convey?

   ....
   ....
   ....
   ....
   ....

3. What **impact** do you want your book to have on the reader?

   ....
   ....
   ....
   ....
   ....

3 Reasons Why People Want to Publish

1. Personal Satisfaction

Many of us dream of publishing a book and for some of us, publishing for personal satisfaction is simply enough. There is nothing like seeing your book in print. The sense of pride and joy you feel can be compared to that of giving birth to your own baby; in fact, the book *is* your very own baby! Having a book to hold and share with your close friends and family is an amazing feeling and inspires other people in your circle to achieve their dreams too.

Personal satisfaction is a worthy reason to print, however, remember that publishing can be costly, so this is truly an investment in realising a dream and leaving a small legacy behind for those you love and generations after.

2. Recognition and Credibility

Publishing a book can be a great way to gain credibility and recognition in your chosen field. Writing a book on a particular specialised subject can help you to create your brand and position yourself as an expert or authority in that area.

Think of your book as a passport to building your client database as well as promoting your company, organisation or services. Your book is not what is going to make you money, but is a tool that adds value to both yourself and your clients. It offers an insight into who you are, what you know and how you can best assist a potential client. If you impress them enough with your knowledge and, more importantly, the value you offer them, they are more likely to buy into you and therefore your products and services.

Publishing a book to support your brand shouts a message loud and clear, "I am here!" Remember, while recognition and credibility are great, it is imperative that what you write offers value.

3. To Share an Important Message/For the Benefit of Other People

Often authors write to share an important and valuable message that will benefit other people. They are passionate about what they have studied or learnt through experience and want to share this with others to enhance their lives. **Conscious Dreams Publishing** loves books that offer value to readers and are designed to benefit other people. Often authors who write for credibility in their chosen field also share the same vision and mission to benefit others with their insight and expert knowledge.

Writing for the benefit of other people does not always mean it must be non-fiction. Books are read for enjoyment and there are plenty of fiction books that bring excitement, a sense of adventure and entertainment. We are living in uncertain times and entertainment is needed now more than ever. When we write from the heart for the benefit of other people, amazing things can magically come to life on the very pages they are written on.

Often authors use their life experiences to share an important message. We all have life experience and what better way to claim our stories and use them to inspire and empower others? When we draw on life experiences and use them to motivate, encourage and inspire, the elevation and healing can literally be felt on every page. It is these types of books that **Conscious Dreams Publishing** is interested in the most.

"When you stand and share your story in an empowering way, your story will heal you and your story will heal somebody else."

Iyanla Vanzant

3 Reasons Why People Fail to Publish

There are three main reasons people fail to publish their inner books. It is not because they are not good or that they wouldn't sell, it is down to three fundamental things that we often allow to trick us into thinking they are good enough reasons to give up our dreams. Do you often hear yourself saying, "It's too hard" or "Someone else will do it better" or "Who wants to hear my story?" Do you find yourself procrastinating and making up excuses or reasons as to why you shouldn't publish your book? I will absolutely guarantee you now that there will be solutions to every single reason and that these are simply myths we create founded within the 'lack' mindset that exists only due to a lack of self-belief, worth and value in what we have to offer. Here are the three main reasons people fail to publish.

1. Lack of Knowledge

Entering the world of publishing can seem like a quagmire. You've spent years writing and perfecting your manuscript and now it's crunch time. There is a plethora of information on the Internet offering a variation of different ways to publish. If you are not well versed in the world of publishing, this can be extremely daunting and an easy place to simply become stuck. It is often on this highway of information that many authors stop due to a lack of clarity, understanding and direction.

My advice is to research, research and research. Become familiar with publishing terms and the different avenues you can take. If you are really passionate about your book, become an expert at it and create a vision for its journey. Writing a book is like having a baby; you have to gain and equip yourself with the key tools, knowledge and resources to raise it. Gaining knowledge is the first step to elevating your book from manuscript to publish.

2. Lack of Money

I can't count the amount of times I've heard someone say, "I can't because of money" or "finances are tight." 'While this may be true, we have to understand that these concepts are first formed in the mind before they manifest into reality.

Publishing a book is costly. I can tell you that because I have been through it. The question you have to ask yourself is, do you really want to publish this book or not? How passionate are you really? Having a dream means achieving it by any means necessary and sometimes we have to get creative about how we achieve that dream; this includes how we fund it. I strongly advise starting a Crowdfunding campaign. I

raised £1,100 in six weeks through setting up a crowdfunding campaign. Contributors donated money in exchange for a copy of the book and other perks. We, in turn, now help other aspiring authors to do the same.

We need to remove the stigma of asking and see it as a valuable exchange. A donation to see your book come to fruition in exchange for the completion of the book is a win/ win situation. You can do a sponsored walk, have a book sale, set up a book club, and/ or have a pre-publish book event and raise money that way. You can seek sponsorship or partner JVs (Joint Ventures) who may pay for advertising space in your book, if you wish to do it that way. There are never ending ways to make money. Money doesn't always have to come from our 9-5.

3. Lack of Belief

We all suffer from fear and doubt at times especially when we are attempting something new. Writing and publishing a book is a huge feat and accomplishment and it is natural to feel uneasy at times. What I will say though is never allow fear or doubt to penetrate your mind. You were born for purpose and if writing and publishing a book is your life-long dream, don't let anything stand in your way. Not even lack of belief.

When fear and doubt tell you "No" you tell them, "YES!" When they tell you, "You can't" you tell them "I CAN AND I WILL." When you feel doubtful or lacking in belief, make sure that you can call on positive people who support you.

Surround yourself with the right people.

Lack of self-belief can be soul sabotaging and the thoughts you tell yourself on a daily basis become our reality. Make sure you are surrounded by people who challenge you, when you are doubtful and support, and celebrate your successes. Their voices, whether positive or negative, will have an impact. Make sure it is positive. Even when you may not feel the part, acknowledge that is where you are, but dress up and show up anyway!

Turn to Page 1–3 in your Workbook

"You cannot climb the ladder of success dressed in the costume of failure."

Zig Ziglar

2. SURROUND YOURSELF WITH POSITIVE PEOPLE

"You are the average of the five people you spend the most time with."

Jim Rohn, American entrepreneur and motivational speaker[3]

Positive Mind.
Positive Vibes.
Positive Life.

Who is in your closest circle? Do they motivate, encourage and inspire you or do they leave you feeling doubtful, insecure and riddled with a lack of self-belief? The people we have around us should enhance us not diminish us. They should facilitate us shining brighter, not act as light dimmers that want to see you shrink back into your comfort zone. They should celebrate your successes and be there for you when you have a '**F**irst **A**ttempt **I**n **L**earning.'

Not everyone will understand what it is that you are doing and not everyone will agree with your choices. But they are your choices and it is your path and if you are striving to be the best version of you and to fulfil your life's purpose and vision, they should support that. **O**prah Winfrey says, 'Surround yourself with only people who are going to lift you higher.'

Studies show that if you place crabs in a bucket and one tries to escape, the others will drag it down. Why? It is a fear of the unknown. They believe the safe place for the crab is the bucket, just like them and that the disappearance (or, in our case, transformation) of the crab will either threaten their own safety and comfort zone or create such a change in the dynamics that the only option is to stop it from escaping.

If the crabs could talk, they would say, "Get back in your place" and "Who do you think you are trying to get out?" If the crab cared to listen long enough, their voices would become its thoughts and eventually it would never try to escape again. If we listen to negative voices long enough, we will start to believe them. They become part of our psyche and belief system.

---

3 https://www.jimrohn.com/

Surround yourself with people who seek to elevate you not drag you down. When you try to achieve great things and life-long ambitions, you will find trials and tribulations, pitfalls and obstacles in what could seem like a maze of a journey, you need a core set of people who value your vision and support you on your journey.

Foster positive relationships with other people and limit the time you spend with those who make you feel negatively about yourself and what you are trying to achieve.

Embrace people and relationships that will elevate your higher, appreciate people who support, motivate and encourage you and do the same for others. What we give out always comes back.

As Plato said, *"People are like dirt. They can either nourish you or help you grow as a person, or they can stunt your growth and make you wilt and die."*

Remember though, nobody can make you wilt without your permission.

Turn to Page 4–9 in your Workbook

*"Surround yourself with people who make you happy.
People who make you laugh, who help you when you're in need.
People who genuinely care. They are the ones worth keeping in your life.
Everyone else is just passing through."*

Karl Marx

3. CREATE A CLEAR VISION

Vision is a key word when publishing a book and must be at the forefront of your mind at all times. We must remember that our book is not simply a way to get our message out there, but also a marketing tool. It is important to think about what we want our book to do for us. Having a book can open many doors so it is essential we know what doors we want it to open.

Having a book allows us to get our message to more people, create links and come face to face with audiences we may never have come into contact with before. Imagine creating a pathway for your book. Where do you want it to go? Nobody wants a book that is stuck on an Amazon or Barnes and Noble shelf hiding among the thousands of other books placed there. How will your book add value? How will people find out about it?

Have a think about what organisations you may want to approach, what JVs (Joint Ventures) you may want to create, what events you wish to speak at or press you can see your book featuring in. Make sure though, that these are all in alignment with your *vision*, *mission*, *why* and *purpose*.

For example, I was approached by a glossy magazine having heard of my book *Mr Wrong*. They wanted me to 'dish the dirt' on exes and send in pixelated images of myself with them to feature in their magazine. Had they read the book, they would have realised that it was not about scandal but more about accepting responsibility for choices we have made and forgiving ourselves to make better choices. While this would have boosted my readership or visibility, it was more important to me to attract the right audience and opportunities that were in alignment with my core values and mission. When you are clear about your values, vision, mission, why and purpose, you will attract the right opportunities for you and weed out the ones that are not. Integrity is key.

Organisations

For example, if your book is about mental health you may wish to contact MIND or Samaritans to assist you with promotion, to talk at your events, feature you in their mailing list. Make sure the collaboration is mutually beneficial to both. In exchange for exposure you could offer them a percentage of your sales or feature them in your book. Think smart!

Make a list of organisations you want to collaborate with.

- ....
- ....
- ....
- ....
- ....
- ....
- ....
- ....
- ....
- ....
- ....
- ....
- ....
- ....
- ....
- ....
- ....

Speaking Engagements

If you are a writer and are used to staying behind the scenes, now is the time to come out of your shell! If you believe you have something powerful enough to share, having a book is great but another powerful way to share and connect with other people is by speaking. You want to share your message with the world, right? Speaking is a great way to connect with people on a more intimate level. It allows people into your world and find out what you really stand for. As writers, we tend to shy away from speaking but it is absolutely paramount if you are to build your platform. Face to face contact is so important, especially if you have a business and want people to buy into your services and products. Remember, people are not simply buying a product they are buying into you.

If speaking is new for you, there are lots of speaking academies offering assistance with confidence and crafting your message. My advice to you would be to sign up with your local Toastmasters. Toastmasters is a non-for-profit organisation that helps you build on and refine your communication, public speaking and leadership skills and a place where you can build support and use the platform to learn invaluable speaking skills, as well as grow in confidence. Check out www.toastmasters.org

Make a list of events you wish to speak at.

- ....
- ....
- ....
- ....
- ....
- ....
- ....
- ....
- ....
- ....

Press

Press Coverage is key. It widens your reach and enhances your credibility. (More about this in Section 6: How to Get Your Book in the Press). You can contact the press by locating the names and contact details of the reporters or particular news desks that are most relevant to you. Usually this information is found at the front or back of magazines or papers. Be clear. Do you want them to feature you and your book or do you want them to write a review? Find out the name of the relevant person to talk to and contact them. The same goes for radio interviews; research the radio station first and contact the relevant person.

Make a list of press outlets you would like to contact. Make a note of names and contact details.

- ....
- ....
- ....
- ....
- ....
- ....
- ....
- ....
- ....
- ....
- ....
- ....
- ....
- ....
- ....

Top Ten Author Success Stories

1. JK Rowling was rejected by 12 publishers before her manuscript *Harry Potter and the Philosopher's Stone*, was accepted by a small publishing house, Bloomsbury. Little did anyone know it would become the bestselling book series in history! Her seventh and final Harry Potter book, *Harry Potter and the Deathly Hallows* broke sales records as the fastest-selling book ever. Her net worth is now $1 billion!

2. After five years of continual rejection, the writer finally lands a publishing deal for her book *Agatha Christie*. Her book sales are now in excess of $2 billion. Only William Shakespeare has sold more.

3. JD Salinger was told, *"We feel that we don't know the central character well enough."* The author does a rewrite and his protagonist becomes an icon for a generation as *The Catcher in the Rye* sells 65 million.

4. Beatrix Potter self-published *The Tale of Peter Rabbit* after relentless rejections. She sold 250 copies. It has now sold 45 million!

5. JK Rowling was a depressed, single mother who wrote her first *Harry Potter* manuscript living in a one bedroom flat. Her last four novels consecutively set records as the fastest-selling books in history, on both sides of the Atlantic, with combined sales of £450 million.

6. *Chicken Soup for the Soul* series by Jack Canfield and Mark Victor Hansen received 140 rejections stating, *"Anthologies don't sell."* The series sells 125 million copies.

7. Are you ready for the most misguided literary critique in history? *"The girl doesn't, it seems to me, have a special perception or feeling which would lift that book above the 'curiosity' level,"* was the critique for *The Diary of Anne Frank*. The book went on to receive a further 15 rejections. Eventually, Doubleday accepts the manuscript and sells 25 million.

8. William Golding received a rejection letter stating that his manuscript for *Lord of the Flies* was, *"an absurd and uninteresting fantasy which was rubbish and dull."* He was rejected more than 20 times. *Lord of the Flies* is now one of Britain's most iconic novels with more than 15 million sales!

9. Little, Brown and Company passes on a two-book deal for Alice Walker. When completed her novel *The Color Purple* sells 10 million and wins The Pulitzer Prize.

10. Louisa May Alcott was told to *"Stick to teaching."* She refuses to give up on her dream. *Little Women* sells millions and is still in print 140 years later. The publisher however, isn't!

Turn to Page 10–11 in Your Workbook

"You may encounter many defeats, but you must not be defeated."

Maya Angelou

Who is in your closest circle?

1. ....
2. ....
3. ....
4. ....
5. ....

Do they motivate, encourage and inspire you?

How would they react if you told them you were writing a book?

Tell them and see.

Notes…

....
....
....
....
....
....
....
....
....
....
....
....
....

Success and the Subconscious Mind

Writing and publishing a book is an enormous feat and an exciting journey. I want this journey to be as positive as possible for you. So first, before anything, we must work on your mindset.

We are multi-dimensional beings made up of mind, body, soul, and spirit. The mind is divided into the conscious, subconscious and the unconscious. Most of the time, we live in our minds; we are either thinking about the past or worrying about the future. Very rarely do we live in the present. All of our thoughts and experiences are downloaded to our subconscious mind on a daily basis. Hour by hour, minute by minute, second by second. But first, what is the difference between our conscious and subconscious mind?

Our mind can be compared to an iceberg. Everything we see at the top (the tip) is our conscious mind. Everything that resides below and hidden is our subconscious mind. Are we programming our minds for success or failure?

Turn to Page 12–39 in Your Workbook

STEP 2: INGRAMSPARK AND ISBNS

Publishing and Distribution

Some people never publish because on the surface, the process seems complicated and drawn out. Though not an overnight process, the process of publishing, once understood, is quite straightforward. Like anything in life, things seem easier once broken down into steps. See image below.

PRE PUBLISHING

Idea

⬇

Plan and structure your book

⬇

Write your book

⬇

Complete first draft

⬇

Give to 5 beta testers to read and offer feedback
(you can create a questionnaire for them with specified questions)

⬇

Commission a professional Script Report

PUBLISHING

1. Create a Clear Vision
Why are you publishing the book? What opportunities do you want to arise? How will you create them?

2. Choose your publisher/platform
The publisher will automatically be linked to a distributor such as Ingramspark. If you are self-publishing you can choose the platform you wish to use. You will use this platform to log your book details, download files, add your account details for royalties, order books and track sales.

Purchase a block of ISBNs
A publisher will provide these. If you are self-publishing, you will have to purchase them.

3. Editing
Your manuscript will be sent to an editor to ensure your manuscript is industry standard and polished.

4. Typesetting
A typesetter will arrange the layout and interior design of your book.

5. Book Cover Design
A book cover designer will create the entire cover based on your vision. You will need a front cover JPEG for your Ebook and full cover — front, back and spine — in PDF (if using Ingramspark.)

PUBLISHING/POST PUBLISHING
These activities should also be carried out and planned pre and during the publishing process.

6. Promotion
Adopt a range of promotional strategies that work for you and think outside the box.

7. Press
In Step 1, you should have created a list of journalists you want to contact to feature your book. Create a press release and/or Media kit to send to them asking them to feature your upcoming book in their magazine, paper, radio, TV show.

Whether traditional or self-publishing, these steps are essential for a successful publication. I advise that you promote before you download your final files onto your platform and order your proof copy. This gives your audience enough time to anticipate your book as well as offer retailers, libraries and booksellers adequate time to decide whether to stock your book ahead of the publication date.

TRADITIONAL VERSUS SELF-PUBLISHING

A few years ago, traditional publishing seemed the only way forward. However, with the rise of technology and increase in digital platforms, self-publishing has become an accepted and respected means to publish your book. The out-dated prejudice that tarred self-publishing as 'vanity publishing', is dissolving as more and more self-published authors are becoming bestsellers, and establishing themselves in the industry.

Authors no longer need to rely on traditional publishers to become successful. However, again I stress the importance of ensuring your book is of the highest quality and that you have a clear marketing and promotion plan in place. There are many pros and cons to both.

Traditional publishing can be tough. It comprises of several steps: seeking an appropriate agent; writing a query email/letter; waiting for a reply; and sending in a sample of your manuscript then waiting anything up to six months before you hear anything. Often unsolicited manuscripts get added to the slush pile and are never seen or heard of again. Make sure the publisher accepts unsolicited manuscripts to save yourself time and unnecessary rejections. However, be aware that few publishers take on new authors without an agent.

Once your manuscript has been accepted, the publisher will be in control of all the publishing processes such as editing, typesetting and cover design, as well as distribution, marketing and promotion. It's important to negotiate how much involvement you will have in regards to the look and feel of your book, as well as the content. Remember you are the author! Publishers will usually pay you an advance fee — an estimation of your royalties for a specific period of time — and they will hold the rights to your book as well as have complete control as to how it is marketed and promoted.

What is great about having a traditional publisher is that they will do most the work for you. They will have access to top quality editors, designers and typesetters, as well as established links within the industry. They, being an established publisher, will be far more likely to get your book on the shelves in internationally recognised bookstores. It is in their interest too!

Self-publishing is, without a doubt, on the increase. It is a great way to establish yourself as an author and learn how the industry works. As a self-published author, you are in control of your book's journey, content, style and promotion. You will hold 100% royalties and have the ability to change your book's details and content quite easily.

If done correctly, this is an empowering way to start out. Once established as a self-published author it is possible that you will be picked up by a traditional publisher who will want to add value and leverage your profile as an author. It's a win/win situation! Many people ask what the differences are between traditional and self-published authors. I have highlighted these in the table below.

Self-Publishing	Traditional Publishing
Will be published under your own publishing brand/self-publishing brand	Will be published under the traditional publisher's brand
Have a direct link to distributors	Publisher will link with distributors
Can edit book details and pricing/wholesale discount	Publisher is in control of book pricing/special offers/wholesale discounts
You have 100% royalty and this is paid into your account every 90 days	Publisher will take percentage of your royalty and pay you, generally, quarterly
Direct link to service providers — editors/cover/designers/typesetters — you can liaise and request modifications	Publisher will have direct link with service providers and request changes on your behalf
Responsible for your own marketing and promotion	Publishing will create marketing campaigns and promote on your behalf
You are responsible for all publishing costs	Publisher will cover publishing costs

Created by Photoangel — Freepik.com

PUBLISHING AND DISTRIBUTION

IngramSpark

As part of the Conscious Dreams Coaching package, you will be set up with an account with IngramSpark. This means you will have a direct link with the distributor of your book. With this account, you will be able to edit your book details at any time, change the pricing, upload updated files, create new titles, calculate your royalties, set retailer wholesale discount, track your sales and royalties and order copies for your book at any given time. Having a direct link with the distributor means you have complete ownership of your book and the ability to track its progress.

Here is an excerpt taken from the IngramSpark Guide to Independent Publishing. It is literally a step-by step guide to the website. Awesome invention! www.bit.ly/IngramGuide

"Welcome to IngramSpark"

"If you were to ask the employees at almost any bookstore in the United States where the books on their shelves came from, they'd likely tell you that most were ordered from Ingram. Established nearly 50 years ago, Ingram Content Group is the largest book distributor in the world, serving 39,000+ book retailers worldwide, of both the brick-and-mortar and the online variety.

Ingram's primary function is to channel books from publishing houses to retailers, but the distributor also owns the world's most technologically advanced print-on-demand company, Lightning Source, which produces books at multiple facilities around the world. In July of 2013, Ingram introduced IngramSpark as a portal for independent publishers and authors to access its print-on-demand services, print distribution channels, and e-book distribution channels. These complementary functions make IngramSpark a true one-stop platform for publishers who want an easy and comprehensive way to bring their books to a national audience."[4]

You will also have the option to promote your book in their catalogue, reaching 90 online retailers and 350+ households.

http://www.ingramspark.com/how-it-works

---

[4] *Taken from IngramSpark Guide to Independent Publishing*

ISBNS

ISBN stands for International Standard Book Number. An ISBN is a 10 or 13-digit number used for identification. An ISBN is unique to every book. It is the best way to find the exact edition of the book you are looking for.

You will need a separate ISBN for each format of your book. In this case, one for your EPUB (Ebook) format and one for your Print On Demand (POD) book.

You can buy your ISBNs separately or in bulk. I strongly advise you buy in bulk because it works out cheaper. Additionally, you will need more than one if you plan to publish in more than one format. Buying in bulk is also much more cost effective if you plan to publish more books.

International Standard Book Numbers are issued in the UK by **Nielsen UK ISBN Agency** and those outside of the UK can purchase from **Nielsen International ISBN Agency**.

About Nielsen Book[5]

Nielsen Book is a leading provider of search, discovery, commerce, consumer research and retail sales analysis services globally. Nielsen runs: the Registration Agencies ISBN and SAN Agencies for the UK and Ireland, ISTC; provides search and discovery products through its Nielsen BookData product range; electronic trading via Nielsen BookNet and PubEasy services; retail sales analysis via Nielsen BookScan; and consumer research through its Books and Consumer Survey.

For more information, visit: www.nielsenbook.co.uk

Nielsen

- Allocates ISBN Publisher Prefixes to eligible publishers based on the information provided by the publisher

- Advises publishers on the correct and proper implementation of the ISBN System

- Maintains a database of publishers and their prefixes for inclusion in the Publishers International ISBN Directory

---

5   Taken from http://www.isbn.nielsenbook.co.uk/controller.php?page=121

- Encourages and promotes the use of the Bookland EAN bar code format
- Encourages and promotes the importance of the ISBN for a proper listing of titles with bibliographic agencies such as Nielsen
- Provides technical advice and assistance to publishers and the book trade on all aspects of ISBN usage.

You can contact them

Tel: +44 (0) 1483 712 215
Fax: +44 (0) 1483 712 214
Email: isbn.agency@nielsen.com
Website: www.isbn.nielsenbook.co.uk

ISBN Price List

Service	Description	Gross Price Including VAT at 20% in £
Single ISBN	Publisher registration, allocation of a single ISBN number. This ISBN is issued by email or can be posted if required, at no extra cost.	£91.00
ISBN Prefix for 10 numbers	Publisher registration, allocation of ISBN prefix plus a list of all 10 associated ISBNs. The list is issued by email or can be posted if required, at no extra fee.	**£169.00**
ISBN Prefix for 100 numbers	Publisher registration, allocation of ISBN prefix plus a list of all 100 associated ISBNs. The list is issued by email or can be posted if required, at no extra fee.	£369.00

You can purchase ISBNs by filling out the application form and returning to Nielsen with your payment details or simply via the online ISBN store at www.nielsenisbnstore.com

Useful Sources of Information

Introductory Publisher's Information Guide

If you are a new publisher these are important notes that guide you through the stages, from purchasing your ISBNs, to registering your title with Nielsen ISBN Agency and distribution. Here's a link to Nielsen's FAQs

www.nielsenisbnstore.com/Home/FAQNew

Applying for an ISBN: What You Need to Know

file:///C:/Users/info/Downloads/ISBN_Guidance_Notes_2012.pdf

Application Form for ISBNs

www.nielsenisbnstore.com/Account/Register

Help Filling out the Application Form

Before filling out the application form, make sure you know the following.

- What your publishing name is
- What trim size you wish to use (size of book — See Chapter 4: Time to Typeset)
- The name of your publisher and distributor
- The formats you require are either paperback/hardback as well as EPUB
- Your distributor is **Lightning Source/Ingram**

Ensure you reflect this on the application form.

Turn to Page 41–44 in Your Workbook

STEP 3: THE EDIT

To Cut or Not to Cut? That is the Question!

THE EDIT

You've finished your manuscript and are ready to go? Writing the manuscript is only half of it. Now it's time for the editing process. The editing process is an interesting one and different manuscripts will require different levels of editing.

When your manuscript is complete, I advise you to send it to five people who you trust and who have time to read it and give you honest feedback. These can be family members, trusted friends or work associates. It's great to get other people's perspectives because often we can become subjective about our own work and it's difficult to separate us, the author, from the intended reader.

Set them a selection of questions that will help you see if…

- your book has had the intended effect…
- is clearly written…and
- the message, plot or character motivations are clear. Sometimes what we think is clear needs more clarification for other people.

The next step after this is the editing process.

There are three types of editing that **Conscious Dreams Publishing** offers. Sometimes we will use one or more of the different types, however, we often use all three. Our editors and proofreaders are of a high quality and always ensure that the book reads with concise clarity and flow, that the meaning is clear and the style is engaging but always in keeping with your author voice. You are the author, the editor's job is to "polish the diamond" that you have produced.

"To write is human, to edit is divine."
Stephen King

Three Types of Editing

Content Editing

This is the first stage of editing and delves deeply to provide qualitative feedback on the subject matter of a manuscript.

In the case of fiction, the editor helps streamline the plot structure, comments on believability, timeline and consistency, character patterns and development, dialogue enhancement, and offers suggestions on various elements of the narrative including removing 'fluff' and 'filler' and ensuring that all scenes are necessary to the story.

For non-fiction the editor will primarily focus on clarity, flow and how to most effectively organise the sections of the book. A non-fiction editor might also comment on consistency of tone and ' filling out' informative text.

Content editing is by far the most intensive and as such carries the highest price tag because it involves a substantial investment of time.

You can also hire a developmental editor who will help you flesh out your idea for the book. A developmental editor will guide you through each portion of your outline, rearrange your outline, as well as suggest characters and plots, red herrings, resources for non-fiction and eventually, where you need to add material.

Copyediting

This is the second stage and includes correcting line errors, but also addresses formatting issues, grammatical errors, fact-checking, and general stylistic consistency. Your content editor may also address these issues.

Proofreading

This is the final stage of editing and involves weeding out all typos, misspellings, and punctuation errors. It is the least rigorous phase and therefore usually the most affordable. A good proofreader is invaluable to your book because, even though it may be a good read, the reader will not be able to see past the typos and errors, making you, the author, and your book appear unprofessional.

Don't get discouraged! Ultimately, your book will be more polished and easier to read as a result of being thoroughly and professionally edited.

The Power of The Cut

I cannot stress enough the importance of the editing stage. This is truly where the magic happens. If your manuscript does not have comments, amendments and tracking marks all over it then you need to rethink about your choice of editor. I am an experienced English teacher who also proofreads essays, short scripts and in the past, books. However, I am never surprised when my manuscript has been revised to ensure clarity and flow or to see that my overlooked typos have been corrected. I would never proofread my own work because the required distance is not there. I can read my manuscript 100 times and still not recognise "the" was spelt "teh" but see it immediately when it is in print and kick myself. Always hire a professional!

The editors on the **Conscious Dreams Publishing** team are experts who will edit your book to the professional and high quality standard you deserve. You will have the contact details of your editor and you will be able to communicate with them directly.

When you finish your coaching with us and, if you chose to go it alone, rehire them. It is worth investing in professionals who can get the job done swiftly and effectively. They will also offer you 10% off if you rehire them. Two of our core values are professionalism and loyalty. We value clients who want to receive professional services. Editing, no matter, which type, is included in the overall pricing of the coaching package.

How to Proceed with an Editor

Once you receive your edited copy of your manuscript, you will find that there may be some comments written in bubbles on a side bar located on the right hand side for you. Once you have read, made changes or agreed with the comments, you can simply delete the comment. Once all comments have been deleted, the right hand side bar will disappear completely. The manuscript will show the track changes and you will have to manually accept the changes as you go through the script. Give yourself a good few hours to do this properly.

Once your manuscript is ready for editing, I will introduce you to your editor. You should really only have to communicate with your editor twice. Once you submit your manuscript and again once you address the comments in their forst edit. You can also arrange to have 1-2-1 zoom calls with some of our editors.

Turn to Page 45 in your Workbook

Sample Content Editing

Here is an example of content editing. You will see that much of the content has been edited to really lift the piece off the paper and give it an added layer of style and flow.

Date Expectations: Content Editing

So the summer months are ~~over~~ gone, ~~but~~ and with ~~it~~ them went~~goesthe Summer of Love. Gone are the days of~~ sunny long dates in the park, ~~walking~~ strolling hand in hand by the riverside and lazy walks by the beach, ~~sun~~ warm rays smiling down at the dating couple beneath. The sun is now replaced with bitter frost, short days and chilly evenings. ~~wherememories~~ Wistful reminiscences of scantily clad women and shirtless men who immersed themselves in the dating game with confidence are now just a whisper in your memory.

Winter months mean hibernation, comfort and rest; a time to retreat from the 'peacock season' of summer. ~~Winter is quite~~ It's a nostalgic time where lovers look back on their past relationships, perhaps with regret, singletons wish they had a lover to cuddle up to and couples make plans for Christmas. It is a time to reflect and also a time to look ~~back on~~ to the year ahead.

~~However,~~Don't be conned by the winter blues, however. Unless you want to put your dating life on stall for several months in the year, the dating game must still go on. ~~Don't be conned by the winter blues.~~ Dating is great during the winter holidays because it gives you the opportunity to be yourself without the added stress of having to show all that skin. So gear up and follow these guidelines for a winter of dating wonder! ~~But first a few tips.~~

Sample Copyediting

Note the comments on the right hand side. These comments are notes to you written by the editor. They are used to communicate with the author about formatting or stylistic changes or suggestions. Comments are not used for every little change but is a great way to communicate and clarify particular choices to the author. For more information about copyediting, go to…

http://www.sfep.org.uk/about/faqs/what-is-copy-editing/

Daniella Blechner Biography: Copy Edited

Daniella Blechner, author of *Mr Wrong*, is a South London based Writer/Director whose real writing journey began by writing comedy sketches for Youth Project *Phenomenon '98* featuring Gina Yashere and Richard Blackwood. She has always been a keen writer and penned her first books, *All The Happy Animals* and *Lucille and her Great Adventure*, at just 8 years old.

At 18 years old she began her career as a performance poet and enjoyed success in bars and clubs in and around London for many years. In 2002 she attended Ravensbourne College where she wrote, produced and directed her first short Connexionswhich was Nominated for Best Screenplay at the BFM Short Film Awards in 2006 and won "Best Open Deck film" when screened at the Cutting East Festival

Daniella won the 2007 Film Fund Award from Lewisham Film Initiative to complete her poetry based short drama, *Hair We Are,* for the Black History Month Short Film Challenge. *Hair We Are* won the 3rd Best Film at the Images of Black Women Film Festival and has been screened at Chicago International Children's film, Pan African Film Festival, LA and BAMKids Film Festival in New York. It was also screened on The Community Channel.

Daniella enjoys examining and reflecting on social issues often laced with a wicked sense of humour. She especially enjoys working with young people and those "at risk" ~~from~~ for exclusion ~~in~~ from society.

Comment [01]: I may be really fine tuning now, but consider using the word "professional" instead of "real".

Comment [02]: …and change this to "creating" since the word "writing" was already used in this sentence.

Comment [03]: Is the word "The" capitalized on the book cover? If not, change it to lower case.

Comment [04]: Add space before "which".

Comment [05]: should—s be capitalized as part of the award title?

Comment [06]: Needs punctuation (period).

Comment [07]: This may be British usage of the word "screened". Do you mean it was "shown" or "aired"? In American English, "screened" means "filtered" or "looked at before time". Just curious.

Sample Proofreading

A proofreader reads the manuscript after it has been edited. It is the final stage and errors are picked up after the manuscript has been edited and before it's published. If we are talking hair, think of content and copyediting as creating the style of the hair and proofreading as the final trim. Great service providers such as the ones we have at Conscious Dreams will do all three; that is, the hairstyle and the trim in one go! For more on proofreading go to…

http://www.sfep.org.uk/about/faqs/what-is-proofreading/

Excerpt from *Mr Wrong*

Severe Commitment-phobes may actually love the woman they are with and fight hard to win her over. However when he eventually gets the woman of his dreams, he can never commit to staying.yetaAt the same time, he is unable to walk away completely. The woman is left feeling totally and utterly confused and may feel she is going insane. I can assure you, you are not. Whilst you may love Mr Commitment-phobe and he you, will he ever be able to provide you with the security and stability your relationship needs?

THE BLURB

Placed on the back of your book, a blurb is a short introductory appetizer to your book. It is a short description of your book designed to entice the reader to want to read more. When making the decision to buy a book, the first thing people will do is, 1. Look at the cover, 2. Read the blurb on the back and 3. If they are interested, browse a few chapter heading and pages inside. The blurb is essential to hook your reader in and get them excited about wanting to open up your book and read it. Don't overlook its power!

Many self-published authors say that writing the book was the easy part; summarising the book in a short, sharp, succinctly effective blurb is another thing entirely!

We may be so attached to our book that it becomes difficult to see it from an objective viewpoint. We may agonise about which part of the message to focus on or, if it's fiction, what part of the plot should be revealed and which characters must be mentioned. The trick about writing the blurb is you want your audience to know just enough to evoke interest and intrigue but not enough to feel as though they have read it already! Engage their attention, then create interest and a desire to read the rest of the book! Less is often more. Most blurbs are between 100-150 words. If your blurb is 300 words plus, you have just written another novel!

For Fiction Authors: 4 Steps to an Irresistible Blurb

According to Digital Book World, a great formula to use for your blurb, if you are writing a novel, is a 4 step process.

1. **Situation** — briefly talk about the general situation of the protagonist (fiction) or the book's theme (non-fiction)

2. **Problem** — what is the sticky situation that's going to be the book's main tension (fiction) or what is the problem this book is going to solve for the reader (non-fiction)

3. **Hopeful possibility** — without giving the answer away, what will your protagonist discover or what will occur that might get her/him out of that sticky situation (fiction) or how will this book give value to the reader and help solve her/his problems (non-fiction)

4. **Mood** — briefly describe the mood of the book: "…a delightful thriller", "a lusty romance", "spine tingling action", "a step-by-step guide to", "a comprehensive how to for the [gardener, cyclist, baker, caregiver]"

For more information, here is a link to this article.

www.digitalbookworld.com/2013/4-easy-steps-to-an-irresistable-book-blurb/

Turn to Page 46 in your Workbook

For a blurb to really work I believe it must be:

- punchy;
- intriguing;
- articulate;
- clear; and
- informative.

If you are writing a non-fiction, 'How-To' or 'Self-Help' book, the blurb must clearly demonstrate what the purpose and function of the book is. The focus must be on what you are teaching your reader and what your message is. Focus on how the reader will feel and what impact your book will have on their lives. Will it make them laugh, will it make them cry, think or even prompt them to approach an old scenario in a new way? What tools and resources are you offering and how can they benefit? Self-development and How-to books should always bring value to the reader. The reader needs an insight into this value from the moment they turn to the back of the book.

For further reading on how to write an effective blurb for a non-fiction book, visit…

http://www.blurb.com/blog/how-to-write-a-blurb-for-your-non-fiction-book/

STEP 4: TYPESETTING

A Time to Typeset

WHAT IS TYPESETTING?

Typeset means to arrange the type or process the data. It has everything to do with the interior layout, down to fonts and spacing to chapter headings and the contents page. Many authors focus on the exterior of their book, however the interior is just as important. Do you really want your reader to read 500+ pages at calibri font 5 and come out needing a stronger pair of glasses than Clark Kent, or Chapter headings that are as inconsistent as Mr Dreamer? (If you've read *Mr Wrong* you would get this joke).

Reading should be an enjoyable experience and the interior should be easy on the eye and the text easy to read. When selecting a typesetter, know that consistency is key.

What does a typesetter do?

When you write your manuscript, it is most likely you are doing so using the A4 letter setting on your computer. Depending on what trim size you have gone for, the typesetter needs to format the file so that it fits the trim size. For example, if your book is 6 x 9 inches then you must tell your typesetter this information so they can format the book appropriately.

A good typesetter will complete the following for you.

1. Use a font style that matches the content

2. Use appropriate line spacing

3. Ensure there is enough white space on the manuscript. Nothing worse than a cramped content squashed on a page! ☺

4. Create a clear and effective contents page

5. Use appropriate headers and footers

6. Create bold chapter headings

7. Ensure the layout is up to industry standard

LAYOUT

When you publish a book, there are certain legal requirements that must be adhered to. For example, every book must have an ISBN and a **Title Verso** page.

The **Title Verso** page is found at the beginning of the book. It will contain all the copyright and publication information including publishing date, company and who owns the rights to the publication. The title verso page is usually found on the second page of the manuscript and the information found there is sometimes referred to as the metadata.

This appears on the left hand side — back side of the first page — in the physical book. It should also contain the title of the book, author's name and genre. The title verso will also indicate whether or not your book is paperback or hardback and, if you have more than one edition, which edition it is. Title verso pages should be half a page and are often written in point 10 and no larger.

The general set up of a title verso page is as follows.

- Book's title and subtitle
- Author, from /book/info/author
- Edition, from /book/info/edition
- Legal text (copyright), from /book/info/legal notice
- ISBN, from /book/info/ISBN

I like to include my web details and contact information in my title verso, but this, or course, is optional.

Example as below.

Mr Wrong: Daniella Blechner.

Non-fiction Personal Development

Copyright © 2014 by Daniella Blechner

All rights reserved. This book or any portion thereof may not be reproduced or used in any manner whatsoever without the express written permission of the publisher except for the use if brief quotations in a book review.

Printed in the United Kingdom

First Printing 2014. Conscious Dreams Publishing.

ISBN: 978-0992991906

www.consciousdreamspublishing.com
www.dingdongitsmrwrong.com

Turn to Page 47 in your Workbook

Layout of a Professional Book

Our wonderful typesetters will ensure your book is laid out professionally. However it is useful for you to know how a professional book of industry standard should read and where each section should be placed.

Let's dissect, delve inside and see exactly how a book is put together, but be mindful that not every part needs to be used or is used by authors.

Bones of a Book

1. **End papers:** End papers, also known as 'leaves' are blank pages which can be found at the beginning and end of a book. This serves as a great space for authors to sign! End papers are more of a hardback feature and aren't often found in paperbacks.

2. **Half Title Page:** Half title pages, also known as 'bastard title' should carry nothing but the title and is the first page readers see. The title is usually halfway down the

page and it serves as a short introduction to the book, or a reminder of the book the reader is reading! ☺

3. **Other books by...** If you have written more than one book, you might choose to list your books here. This page should appear on the other side of the half title page. Alternatively, it could have its own page.

4. **Title Verso Page:** As discussed above, this page carries the title, author, ISBN and publication information as well as the copyright notice.

5. **Dedication Page:** It's a lovely idea to dedicate your book to someone who has supported you along your journey or to someone who you hold close in your memory. This page is dedicated purely to dedications (like what I did there?) and no other information should be on this page. The best dedications are the ones that come from the heart.

6. **Acknowledgements:** These can go either after the dedications, Table of Contents or at the back of the book. This is usually down to the publisher's preference, or in this case, yours. This is a great space to thank those directly involved in the project such as the publishing house, writing coach, agent or editor. It is a great space to also thank loved ones who have supported you along the way. It's a fun idea to try to link the theme of your book in your acknowledgements. For example, if you are writing a memoir, how did a particular person contribute to the fantastic person you are today?

7. **Table of Contents (TOC):** If you want the posh industry term, you can impress your peers by using the term TOC. (Just when you thought the world was full of enough acronyms!) Today, the TOC page is generally used for nonfiction books and simply lists the sections of the book, including the dedication and acknowledgements pages. A children's chapter book might include a TOC listing each chapter.

8. **List of Illustrations, Charts, Photos and Diagrams:** Visual aids that support the information given in the text should be listed on this page. If the images are purely used for comedic value and do not need to be referenced, then this page is not necessary.

9. **Foreword:** This is a piece written about you and about your book. It is written by someone who knows you and can testify who you are and what you do. Forewords are usually written by well-known figures who may also be published. Think carefully

about who you will choose for your foreword. If you are writing a relationship book, don't get a comedian to write your foreword. Get someone who is in alignment with your topic. For example, if you are writing a book about forgiveness then a high profile public figure like Ilyana Vanzant would be ideal! And if you manage to get her to write your foreword, I will personally put on a celebratory party in your honour! The foreword is usually broken down into three parts;

- The writer of the foreword should **establish how they know you** and came to write the foreword. This establishes credibility and distinguishes the relationship between both yourself and the person you have selected to be your writer.

- **Introduce the problem the book intends to solve**. Statistics and facts can be used here. The writer should draw a comparison between the topic and how they relate to that topic. This establishes links and creates clarity and credibility. They can also identify how the author has helped to address the problem, the importance of the work they are introducing or mention author credentials relating to the topic at hand.

- The last part should be about the **impact on the readers**. How will the book transform them? What impact will it have and how will the reader feel once the book has been read? The Foreword is like the warm up act before the main act and should prepare the reader for an exciting and enjoyable read.

NB: Forewords should be no longer than 1,000 words.

10. **Preface:** This is written by you and contains information about the book. You can talk about your inspiration behind your chosen topic and how it personally relates to you and what significant impact the information will have on the reader.

11. **Front Matter:** All the pages listed above are known as the Front Matter and all page numbering uses Roman Numerals. After this point the pagination — standard page numbers — starts and we are on our way with the book's content!

12. **Introduction:** You have been introduced by your foreword writer and the contents page, dedications and acknowledgements have geared them up for the main course, now this is the time to introduce yourself. What makes a good introduction? Speak directly to the reader, forge a relationship and let your personality shine through as you introduce your book and the book's topics. Include why you have chosen to write about this topic and how it relates to you. Share something special with the

readers, an anecdote or personal information. The aim is to build a connection from the beginning.

13. **Body or Chapters:** This relates to the text of the book. Nonfiction books are usually broken down into sub-titled chapters, which are referenced in the TOC. However, in fiction segments may be referred to as scenes and not referenced in the TOC.

14. **Back Matter:** Similar to Front Matter, this refers to all the pages that appear at the back of the book after the main body of work. These pages are usually given page numbers too.

15. **Afterword:** This contains any additional information the reader may wish to know. For example, if you are writing about the life of an adopted tiger, readers might want to know how the tiger will be released back into the wild in the future.

16. **Appendices:** This includes any sources of information that support the book's topics. For example, a list of recommended reading, useful websites, list of organisations or useful helplines.

17. **Glossary:** Usually only found in nonfiction books, a glossary lists vocabulary and words that relate to the book's topic, along with the definition.

18. **Bibliography:** Lists the references used in the book's research.

19. **Index:** Usually found in nonfiction books, the Index is an alphabetical list of significant terms found in the text, as well as the pages they appear on. This is a great help for those seeking specific information.

20. **Author Biography:** This is where you talk about you. This should be a short paragraph or page about you detailing who you are and what you have achieved. You may want to add your personality to it with a random fact about yourself, or briefly explain what drove you to write the book. Your *Why*!

21. **End Papers:** These are those lovely blank pages at the back of the book that simply give your book some air. Think about it as someone dropping the mic after a phenomenal speech! Congratulations, you are done!

Turn to Page 48–49 in your Workbook

STEP 5: BOOK COVER

How to Create a 'Drop the Mic' Book Cover

FORGET WHAT YOU HAVE BEEN TOLD!

We've all heard of the phrase 'Never judge a book by its cover.' Well, when it comes to publishing your book, forget that! Looks matter. The exterior of your book only has one chance and one chance only. It has one chance to grab the reader's attention; it has one chance to stand out among the other books; and one chance to clearly tell the story of the book inside. What makes a brilliant book cover and what is a cover comprised of?

Breaking Down the Cover

A book cover is broken down in a few parts.

1. **Title:** This must be big, bold, attention grabbing and easy to read from a distance of about 6 metres.

2. **Subtitle/shout-line/tagline:** This is a cleverly worded line that supports your title.

3. **Image:** The image is crucial; it supports and represents your entire book. It should be balanced and professionally composed.

4. **Author's Name:** You can choose to have your name boldly spread across the book, at the top or at the bottom. This is a matter of individual taste.

5. **Reviews:** It's a great idea to get an appropriate and relevant public figure or a media review to add credibility to your book.

6. **Awards:** Any awards you have won from your previous books can be mentioned on the cover. In addition, if you win any awards or achieve bestseller status, you can use the logo on your book. Again, this is a matter of personal choice.

MY BOOK COVER STORY

In my naivety, I thought creating the book cover would be a doddle and so I continued to write the book without thinking much of it. I had a general idea in my head and that was enough. I am a very visual person. However, I am not the world's greatest drawer, nor did I know the difference between vector image and illustration, so getting my idea across can be tricky at times. It took a few months to find the right designer who understood my vision and could translate it beautifully into a front cover I am proud of. Her name is Sunny Tellone and she is based in Los Angeles.

As my book is about love and relationships and an element of unavailability, I wanted the cover to reflect this. I wanted a cover that used symbolism, to not only attracted the potential reader's attention, but also inform the reader about the predicament many women face when loving the Emotionally Unavailable Mr Wrong.

For example, my cover comprises the following.

- **Author Name:** Written in a stylistic font on a red strip background.

- **Title:** Which is thick, squared, bold, red lettering because I wanted something bold and in your face.

- **Vector Image:** I asked for a silhouetted vector image of a man and a woman. The woman wears a red dress and is leaning towards her Mr. Wrong with her head tipped back and arms stretched back. I asked for a girlish looking woman who has a fun yet vulnerable energy. The man is dark and mysterious. His body language is standoffish, yet cool. We can tell that he is not as into her as she is into him and behind his back he hides his heart.

- **Colour Scheme:** Simple red, white and black.

- **Symbolism:** There is plenty of symbolism in this cover. The body language symbolises unrequited love or an imbalance in a relationship; one will give her heart freely, the other has no intention of even allowing a glimpse of his heart.

The mirroring of the M and W symbolise the behaviour of the couple. Their behaviour towards each other is a mirror of unresolved issues. The heart wrapped in barbed wire motif represents an inability to love or a guarded heart. Mr Wrongs aren't born, they are made, therefore the barbed wire symbolises being hurt or wounded too.

- **Subtitle:** For nonfiction we use the term subtitle; for fiction, terms such as shout-line or tagline are often used. My subtitle is *Learn from Mr Wrong and Claim Mr Right*. With such a controversial title as *Mr Wrong* I wanted to inform readers that the book is about self-discovery and learning from our patterns and encounters with Mr Wrong rather than berating him.

Mr Wrong Cover c/o Sunny Tellone

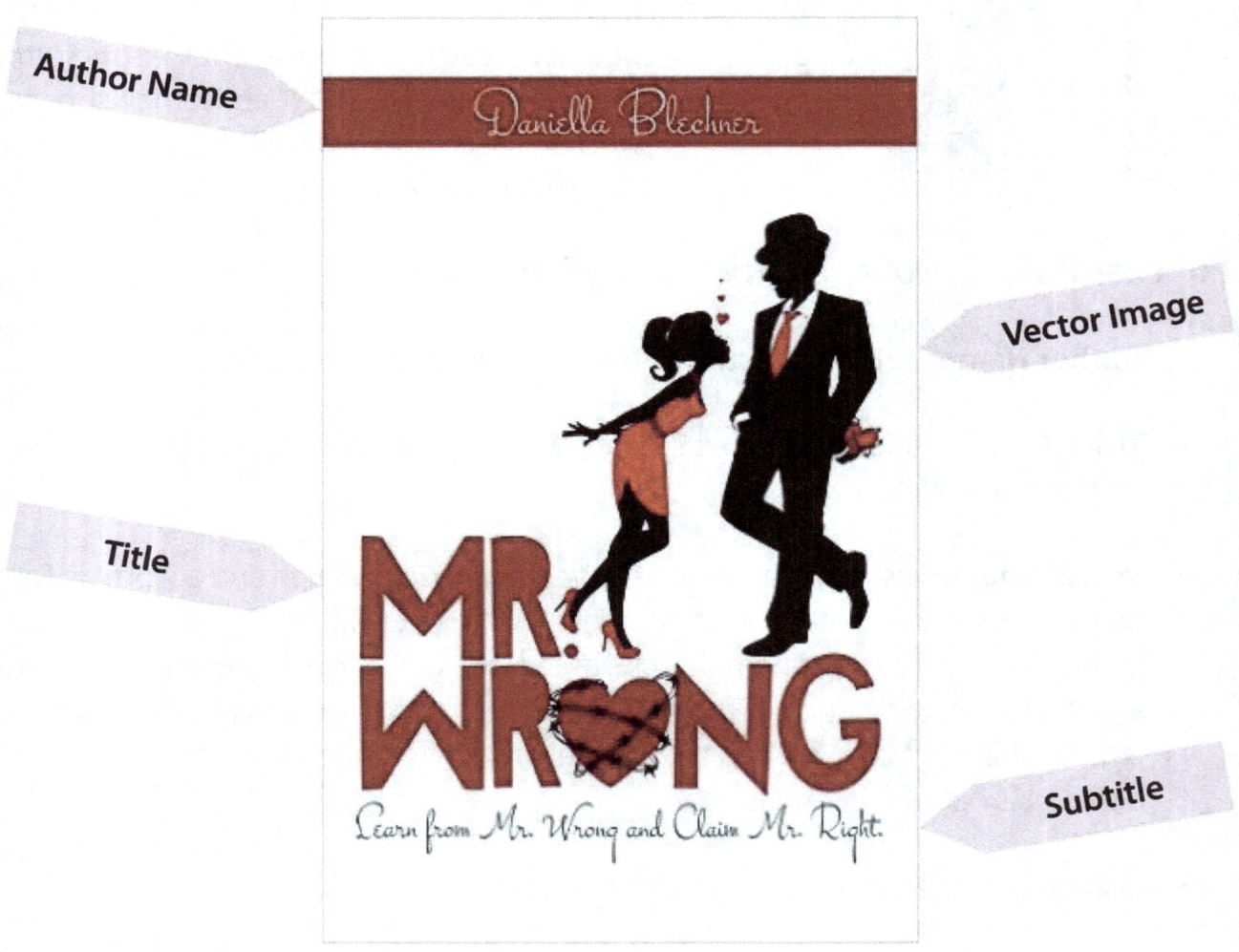

Turn to Page 51 in your Workbook

DECIDING ON YOUR CONCEPT

Having a clear vision is essential when deciding on the look and feel of your book. It is important that you can clearly convey your ideas to the cover designers. **Conscious Dreams Publishing** knows that vision is important, which is why during the Vision Creation Session you will work together with me, to draw out and establish a vision for the look and feel of your book. We focus on the message you want to convey and the book's Value Proposition[6] so we can clearly target the right audience and market your book effectively. To make communication easy when dealing with the artists, you will be given a standard form to fill out when requesting your book cover, as below.

Name of Book: ....

....

Subtitle: ....

....

Author Name: ....

....

Colour Scheme: ....

....

Layout: ....

....

Image Details: ....

....

Once the final cover has been completed, you can request tweaks because the package is subject to a maximum of three revisions.

---

[6] *An innovation, service, or feature intended to make a company or product attractive to customers.*

TOP 10 TIPS TO A 'DROP THE MIC' BOOK COVER

I used this phrase earlier, but what do I mean? 'Drop the Mic' refers to excellence. Imagine listening to a powerful speech; so powerful you are moved into action. It might be a speech urging you to fulfil your dreams, a motivational speech or a speech that makes you want to get up and enjoy the life we have been blessed with. That truly is a speech with impact. The speech indeed is so powerful that the speaker no longer needs to speak...all that is left for them to do is, simply...Drop the Mic!

That is what your cover should do. It speaks for itself and is the key to attracting a potential reader to pick up your book, open it and buy it! Let's create a Drop the Mic cover for you, right now!

1. Create a bold title that grabs the attention of the reader.
2. Use quality stock images not cheap or free clip art from Microsoft!
3. Have a clear vision and make sure the cover reflects the book genre.
4. Create a punchy subtitle that gives readers more information about your book and its message.
5. Don't over complicate the fonts; no more than two is advisable.
6. Use a strong image that communicates the heart behind the book. It is not a great idea to feature main characters on the book cover; best to leave that to the reader's imagination.
7. Keep it simple. Ever heard the phrase 'less is more'? Definitely true when it comes to book covers. A cover should convey a quick and easily digestible message that acts as a first port of call before opening. Too much detail can be off putting.
8. Make sure any images have been cleared for copyright.
9. Research Top 10 book covers in your book genre.
10. Test the model. If you can draw, have a bash at sketching a few different types. Similarly, you can explain the concepts to friends and family and ask them which they would feel more compelled to pick up. Market research is key. Your audience matters.

Good luck! ☺

Turn to Page 52 in your Workbook

STEP 6: PROMOTION

7 Ways to Promote Your Book

What is promotion?

Many authors publish books but sales remain low. Why? It is because of a lack of promotion. Many authors think that publishing a book is enough to attract readers, it isn't. Promotion is absolutely imperative to enhancing your sales and distribution. But first, what is promotion?

Promotion is the marketing and advertising of a product, service or brand. The aim is to gain customer awareness, generate sales and create customer loyalty.

Why promote?

People will not know your book exists unless you tell them it exists. It is important to promote your book to first, ensure your book is visible in an ever growing market and secondly to grow your platform and market. Promoting your book to the right audience will not only increase brand awareness, but help to establish you as an authority in your field. It will help you gain loyal customers who will not simply buy into the book, but also what you have to offer, whether that is workshops, further books, products and services, events, coaching or further. Promoting is about growing your niche, creating advocates and building your platform.

Whose role is it to promote?

I speak with many authors who say they have signed up with publishing companies and are disappointed due to lack of sales. They pinpoint this as a result of the publisher not constantly promoting. If you publish with **Conscious Dreams Publishing**, we will naturally promote your book as well as offer press opportunities as we see fit.

However, if you pay for a company to simply publish your book, then that is all they will do. Although we may assist with promotion, I am a staunch believer that there is no better advocate for your book than you. You are the author, you know your why, vision, mission and purpose better than anyone. Therefore, you are responsible for promoting and pushing your book forward.

Don't think you have to be salesy or that there is a formula to it, have fun with it and be creative. You can pay Public Relations companies to generate press and you can pay various companies to promote, but remember, people buy people not products and the audience want to connect with you.

How long should I promote for?

The first year of a book's life is the most important. It is during this time that you are building your platform and gaining readership. Have a six month to a year promotion plan to keep your book fresh in the market while it is current. There is never a time to stop promoting but if you want to build your platform, ensure that you do not leave it too long in between books. Keep your books current and continue to offer your readers more value. This will mean that as your value and your body of work increases, the focus will change to what is current. Once buyers buy into what is current, they will be more inclined to buy your previous work.

Now, let's get going. I want to offer you 7 creative ways that you can promote your book, which connects you to your audience with heart, as opposed to the obvious salesy, spammy and pushy options that create more of an impersonal feel. Remember, everything you do should be about connecting.

7 WAYS TO PROMOTE YOUR BOOK

1. Endorsements and Reviews

Endorsements and reviews are crucial for books. They enhance the credibility of your book and create a sense of reassurance for the potential reader. Now, it may be tempting to send your book to anyone and everyone to review but this is the wrong approach. You need to create a focused list of specific people your book is aimed at, as well as key figures and influencers in your chosen field. If you are writing a book about Conscious Parenting, find people of influence within that field. Shortlist celebrities or well-known figures who practise this or source psychologists, authors and experts, within this field to write a review. This not only backs up your own expertise, but tells the reader that your book is worth buying and that your book has credibility. It builds that know, like and trust factor. That sense of *"Well, if Oprah Winfrey says it's a page-turner it must be!"* Gather reviews before your book is published by sending a PDF of your edited manuscript so you can add these inside your book or on the back. Don't be afraid to contact press too. Wouldn't a review from *The Times* or *Guardian* be great? It is worth a try!

Getting a key influencer or well-known figure to endorse your book, does not always mean they have to write a review. They could simply tweet about it, post about it or simply have a picture taken with you and your book. It is little effort on their behalf and if you get them to see the value in what you are offering, it is amazing what a retweet from a well-known figure can do! Face the fear and do it anyway, contact them, offer them a copy of your book and follow up to see what they thought. Be bold in asking for an endorsement.

2. Twitter Party

Now this sounds exciting, I know. A Twitter party is exactly that. People nowadays have online launches, however, I am still and will always be a fan of in person events and launches. Having an online launch or Twitter party is a great idea because it connects people from all across the world and focuses them on your book. Arrange a Twitter party by letting all of your Social Media contacts and mailing list know that you will be launching or having a party online and adding your Twitter handle to attend. Tell them the day and time to attend along with a hashtag they can use to find the discussion about your book. You may want to set a particular topic for your book. For example,

"Are Mr. Wrongs born or made?" and get a great discussion going online that can be followed using the hashtag #MrWrong. Remember to have links to your book or create memes with the weblink. It's a great way to get a discussion going, create engagement and build an online following. Get Twittering!

3. Create Your Book Cover

Creating your book cover ahead of time is a good idea because it gives you time to promote. Use your book cover to announce the publication date of your book and create posts, social media banners and adverts using the cover to create anticipation and visibility. Get your potential readers used to seeing the cover and create a sense of excitement and buzz around it. You can use the cover to accompany your blogs, as well as in media kits and press releases that should include your relevant book information. Using your book cover to promote the book is a great visual statement.

4. Merchandise

Creating merchandise is another great way to promote your book. Think beyond simply selling your book. What innovative and creative ways can you engage your potential readers. Can you create bookmarks with quotes or facts about your subject matter? Can you have interactive competitions about them? How about calendars, mugs, bags or postcards? Remember these are all great ways to promote your book. Imagine a reader walking down the street with a *Mr Wrong* bag saying, "Have you seen Mr Loose Eye? Stay away!" Would that grab people's attention? Inject some humour into it too. On the day of my launch I gave away 20 *Mr Wrong* stress balls and they are still in demand! Be creative, fun and inventive.

5. Run a Kindle Countdown Promotion

Kindle Promotions are a great way to draw attention to your book. A Kindle Countdown Promotion is when you set your Kindle Ebook to a discounted price for a set period of time on Amazon. You can set your book for as little as 99p and raise the amount each day in small increments until your book is back to the original price. Consumers will be able to see the original price and time left on the Countdown Promotion. If you are enrolled in the Kindle Select Programme, you can also set your book for free for a period of time. If you are using the Kindle Countdown facility via Kindle Select, be aware that you will only be able to distribute your book using the Amazon platform and no other for a period of 90 days. Note that you can easily change the price yourself using your Kindle Direct Publishing account and restore back to the original price after a set period of time. The aim of this promotion is to drive as many people as you can to that particular site to buy your book for a limited period of time only. Why? What a lot of people do not know is that one of the secrets to becoming a bestseller, not within your category, is that it is time sensitive. If you shift more books in comparison to other people in that particular category at a particular time than you can climb the sales ranks quickly. What better way to do that than by running a Kindle Promotion on special occasions — day of publication or launch is a great one — to help you climb the ranks within your category? It is a great incentive for people to buy and, hey, everyone loves a good deal! For more info, visit www.tinyurl.com/kindlepromo7

6. Blogging

Blogging is a great way to connect with your audience. Although I am not a fan of *50 Shades of Grey* at all, it cannot be denied that the power of blogging turned out to be extremely lucrative for EL James. Many books first start out as blogs and this is a great way to build your platform and gain a following. I started *Mr Wrong* as a blog, displaying different characters, blogging about themes covered in the book and posting extracts from it. I also kept my audience informed as to the progress of the book and invited bloggers to share their own stories. The key to blogging is connecting with other bloggers and making them feel like a part of your journey. Use the search button to find bloggers who blog about your topics by typing in keywords, follow them and comment on their blogs. You will find this will help you to develop relationships and establish connections by sharing contacts and commenting. It may feel time consuming to start with but it's absolutely worth it, especially if you can create opportunities such as asking bloggers with large platforms to blog about your book. Always make it a fair exchange. Think about what you can offer for them in return. Can you reblog their posts, refer to them and direct your platform to their blog? Perhaps you can guest blog for their platform. Everything is about reciprocity and relationship building. Blogs are great for this. You can also create links to your blogs in your newsletters too.

7. Livestreaming

Livestreaming is a great way to gain new audiences but also an intimate way to allow potential readers to get to know you. Livestreaming is when you broadcast live to an audience in real time. You can use platforms such as Facebook Live, YouTube Live, Twitter, Linkedin and Instagram Live, to do this. You can use livestreaming to establish who you are, what your message is and what your book is about to a live audience. There are many ways you can use this platform to elevate your book. You can do this by talking about topics you cover in your book to create a real-time discussion, informing your audience of events, special offers and promotions you are running, as well as use it to talk about other services you offer. Remember though that the key again, is to connect with your audience, not sell. Create discussions, gain interest, provide value and significance, share your story and don't be afraid to show the audience who you are. Many of us hide behind keyboards or digital marketing but there is nothing better in my view, than seeing someone in the flesh, whether this is in person or via the cyber waves to create that connection. Believe me, I was one of these people who liked to hide behind the scenes but since I started using livestreaming in 2016, I have created more connections and more clients than before getting in front of the lens. If confidence is an issue or if you are not sure where to start, I highly recommend that you connect with my very first Book Journey mentee, Janine Cummings who is now The UK's Number 1 Female Livestreamer and Social Media Strategist. You can connect with her at www.janinecummings.tv

Turn to Page 53–55 in your Workbook

YOUR BOOK LAUNCH

Your book is complete, your baby has arrived and the day has come. Your book is about to be launched. During our Vision Discovery Session, you visualised your book launch. Visualisation is important because it creates a clear image in your mind as to how you envision your book launch. It is also important to have an outline for the day so the launch is well organised and runs efficiently.

Questions to Consider

1. What sort of book launch do you want to have?
   A reading, author talk, networking, or a debate

2. What sort of venue do you want to use?
   Library, cafe, bookstore, bar, community hall, or restaurant

3. What is your budget?
   Account for everything before you book anything

4. What extra added value are you offering your guests?
   Catering, goodie bags, special offers

5. What special offers are you promoting on the day?
   50% off second book, merchandise, Kindle promotion on day of publication, see bestseller document

6. How can you stay in contact with your guests?
   Mailing list, or card jar

7. Make a list of things you need on the day
   Photographer, videographer, clipboard, projector, chairs

Turn to Page 56–60 in your Workbook

ULTIMATE GOAL

Remember your ultimate goal is to promote your book and gain a following. You want your audience to tell as many people as they can about your amazing book. A top tip is to use merchandise to advertise your book. This can be a bookmark, mug, bag or postcard, which your attendees can either buy or win during a raffle. Use postcards to promote your special offer.

Set your book launch date before your book is officially published. Create a Kindle promotion on the day of publication and plug the publication date and promotion throughout the launch. Share your website and social media handles and ask your attendees to tweet, blog and post about your book and share your special offer like mad on the day of publication. Social media is a great way to promote your book.

STEP 7: PRESS

How to Get Your Book in the Press

PUBLIC RELATIONS FOR YOUR BOOK

Promoting your book should be a consistent effort. The first year of your book's life will be the most important. It is a great idea to create a database of press contacts and journalists and pinpoint, which contacts are:

- relevant to your book. There is no point in contacting *The Financial Times* asking them to feature your book *50 Shades of Karma Sutra*; and

- in alignment with your brand. This is where your values, beliefs and integrity come into play. As I mentioned earlier, my book, *Mr. Wrong* is about celebrating our experiences by learning and growing from them. I was asked by a women's magazine to send in a real life dish-the-dirt story along with photos of my exes pixelated and I said, "No." That level of exposure and focus on the negative evoked a sense of shaming that did not resonate nor reflect the values or integrity of what the heart of my brand or book represented. Always stay true to you. Not every opportunity is golden.

TOP 10 TIPS FOR APPROACHING PRESS

1. Find out the name of the person you are contacting!

The press get hundreds of emails a day promoting organisations, events, products, authors, movers and shakers, so it's important to be noticed. People will always respond to a personal touch rather than a blanket email entitled, "Dear Sir/Madam" or "Hi!"

2. Find out what that person and brand like

You want the person to be interested in you and your product so it is vital to show interest in them. What attracted you to choosing *The Voice* over *The Daily Mail*? Was there an article in there that interested you? Do you or your book have anything in common with the person you are writing to? Mention it. For example: *"As a lover of bikes, I thought you might be interested in my book XXX. The lead character rides a Ducati Monster!"*

3. Write an innovative email title

Instead of writing a blanket email entitled; the name of your book in the name of magazine/newspaper etc., use your research to find out more about the person and brand. To mark the end of 2015, I had a full page spread interview featuring my book *Mr Wrong*. How did I do it? I found an article in The Mail Online based on relationships and I entitled it Re: *Jo, I loved your article; Why Men Cheat*. I went on to tell her about my book and I received an instant reply. This approach has worked far better than *"Mr Wrong* in *The Daily Mail."*

4. Three Things: Who, What and Why

Send three short paragraphs that succinctly answer these questions.

1. Who You Are?   2. What You Do?   3. Why People Should Care?

You have a short space of time to present who you are and what your 'noble intention' is. Connect to the person you are writing to. How can your book assist, contribute and add value to other people in a way that similar products cannot. What makes your book different?

5. Press Release

A press release is an official statement issued to newspapers and media outlets about an event, service or product. In this case, your book. If you chose to sign up with a PR company they will write you a professional press release and send it to contacts in their media database. They will be responsible for scheduling interviews, meetings and getting you features for radio, magazines, TV, newspapers and blogs. Alternatively, if you are on a budget, or if you prefer, you can do your own PR with the database we provide or by sourcing contacts through your own networking and research. Some people say that press releases are out-dated and the press now prefer a more personal approach. My belief is that it is good to have one just in case because it is a professional CV for your book and you never know who may ask for one at short notice.

6. Attachments

In my experience, journalists don't often like an email with lots of attachments and information to download. Make it easy for them. Perhaps include links to blogs, excerpts of your book, an interview and copy and paste your press release into the body of the email. You can always send headshots and manuscripts once engaged.

7. Have Hope and Follow Up

Now that you've fired off your emails, be patient and wait for a reply. While waiting, have hope and faith that what you have to offer is of value and that the media you have contacted can benefit from what you have to offer on their show/magazine/paper, etc. Remember though, that they receive hundreds of requests a day so it is important to follow up. A polite email such as,

Dear Joanna Blogs,

I hope you are well. I recently contacted you in regard to my book Mr Wrong. Have you had a chance to read it yet? I would love for you to consider featuring Mr Wrong (the book, not the man!) on your show.

Have a great day

Daniella

8. Contact Details

Remember to attach your contact details under your signature such as phone number, blog and website and, if you wish, any nominations of awards you have received. It gives extra information about you and allows the recipient to follow you on social media and check out your links!

9. Demonstrate Credibility

Remember journalists get inundated with all sorts of requests from people wanting them to cover their business, product, service or story. If you are writing a book to leverage your business or to highlight an important cause, demonstrate credibility. This point links back to the promotion for your book. If you have a key influencer or a well-known figure who has reviewed your book, this will enhance your credibility. Having links to other press features will also help. If you have teamed up with another credible organisation — known as a Strategic Alliance — such as Cancer Research, you can mention this as by association. It will set you apart from other people and increase your authority.

10. Editorial Features List

Most media outlets will have an Editorial Features List. This list is literally a calendar schedule of what content and themes will be published each week/month. This is a great way for you to ascertain when and where your feature best fits. A tip is to contact the Features Editor and ask more specifically what they are looking for in that particular issue. For example, if the theme for February is *relationships* and your book is about *cars* then February is not a great time to request a feature. If however, your book is based on this particular topic or area, you are in luck! From here, you can discuss your story and see if it is something that fits. Taking care to find out what they want exactly for a particular issue or month creates an instant connection and avoids wasting time, sending in information, requests for features at a time that is inconvenient or irrelevant to your topic. Research goes a long way!

Turn to Page 61–62 in your Workbook

BONUS MATERIAL

Securing Retailers

It's important to remember that publishing your book is only the beginning. Establishing the life you want for your book means deciding what retailers you want to stock your book. Having a published book does not automatically gain you rights to have your books stocked in bookstores and libraries. There is a process and, if the truth be told, self-published authors are competing with big names and publishing companies, but does it matter? No, however, tenacity and thinking outside of the box is a must!

Why approach retailers?

While your book will be available online in both Print and Ecopy formats, having your book in bricks and mortar retailers increases your visibility, as well as your credibility. It will open up and widen your audience. It is also a great opportunity to forge successful relationships with retailers and establish your authority as an author. This will make them more inclined to promote and market your book.

Before securing your books in bookstores, there are many things to consider.

1. **Wholesale Discount:** Bookstores will want to purchase your book at a 40% discount or more. With IngramSpark you can set your discount between 55% and 30%.

2. **Returns Policy:** Taking an unknown author's book and stocking it on their shelves is a big gamble. Therefore retailers will often not accept proposals that offer a no return policy. Retailers often do not accept books from Amazon KDP (formally known as Createspace) due to this. Ensure that you enable the Return option on your IngramSpark account.

3. **Competitors:** You are competing with mainstream publishers and well-known authors for shelf space.

4. **Target the Right Retailers:** Ensure you are targeting the right retailers for your book genre. There is no point in sending in a proposal or Advanced Information Sheet for your book about train spotting to an erotic bookstore!

5. **Relationships are Key:** Build a relationship with your local bookstore and adopt a personal approach.

Gathering Reviews

Gathering reviews for your book is a great way to build credibility and authority in your field. Carefully select influential public figures and organisations who are respected in your field of expertise and simply approach them to write a review and endorse your

book. What is the worst that can happen? They say, 'No' What happens then? You keep going. Keep promoting and proving that your book will sell well and that there is an audience out there who cannot wait to buy your book.

Remember many successful authors were told, 'No' before they became hugely successful. 'No' is what makes us stronger. Having strong reviews from experts will increase the, 'Wow factor' and make your book more attractive or appealing to retailers. "Well, if Steve Harvey says *Mr Wrong* is a must buy, I guess we better stock it!" I hear the manager in Waterstones Head Office saying.

Wholesale Discount

My suggestion to first time authors is to set your discount between 55% and 40%. This is to establish a good working relationship with the retailer. They are buying from you for the first time and taking a risk with an unknown author. Therefore providing them with a decent wholesale discount and returns policy not only adds security but may encourage them to purchase more of your books in bulk.

Everything in the first instance is about fostering a good working relationship. Once your book proves it can sell well, the retailer will be more likely to accept a lower discount and buy more.

Advantages of being an Indie Author

There are many advantages to being an indie author. What mainstream publishers do not have that you have, is the ability to have a personal approach. You are the author of your book; you have put in the work and know the heart of your book inside out. You are in a great position to establish a relationship and rapport with your local bookstores, libraries and retailers. Pop in, find out who oversees events at the bookstore, tell them about your book and organise an author talk. Promote and market your event like mad and demonstrate to the bookstore that there is an audience for your book. How do I know this? I tested this idea. I organised a fantastic book event as part of a book tour at Croydon Waterstones, who ordered a batch of my books in bulk and eventually displayed *Mr Wrong* in the window! The book, not the man!

Turn to Page 63 in your Workbook

In life we have to be bold. My motto is, *"Be bold or forever live wondering if..."*

What's your motto? ....

Importance of an Advanced Information Sheet

If you are contacting retailers ahead of time many may ask for an Advanced Information Sheet (AI Sheet). An AI Sheet is your book's blueprint. It is a one-page sheet that contains all the relevant information a retailer needs to know about your book such as: the title; tagline; genre; word count; ISBN; synopsis; and available formats etc. For sales reps it is a critical selling point that allows retailers to understand a very quick and snappy feel for your book. AI Sheets can be sent at least three months in advance. For example, my AI Sheet is on the next page.

Turn to Page 64–65 in your Workbook

ADVANCED INFORMATION SHEET

ADVANCED INFORMATION SHEET

Title: Mr Wrong

Author: Daniella Blechner

Keywords: Dating, relationships, love

BIC CODE: VFVG

Size: 6 x 9

Page Extent: 296

Publication Date: 20th September 2014

Format: Paperback

ISBN: 9780992991906

Price: £12.99

Language: English

Publisher: Conscious Dreams Publishing
www.consciousdreamspublishing.com

Blog: www.dingdongitsmrwrong.com

Contact: daniella'consciousdreamspublishing.com

Selling Points:

- Sneak peeks into real life relationship stories and witty dating disasters
- A Mr Wrong manual!
- Exercises, quizzes, questionnaires designed to engage the reader interactively and self-discover
- A balance of humour, poignancy and self-exploration
- Men have their say too!
- No preaching, teaching or rules!

Summary

Do you ever feel as though you will never meet the right man? Are your relationships leaving you wondering what you're doing wrong? Do you attract the same type of man, repeating the same negative patterns over and over again? If you find yourself thinking 'Here we go again' or 'I've been here before', if you're dating men who love you and leave you emotionally wounded and insecure, or if you're wondering why you just can't seem to get it right, I have news for you. You are simply dating the wrong men.

Mr. Wrong is an insightful and witty exploration as to why some women continually attract the wrong men. This powerful collection of humorous, insightful, and entertaining stories are written by women from across the world that have encountered and overcome toxic Mr. Wrong relationships.

The book is designed to unite, inspire, and empower women through interactive quizzes, exercises, and meditations. Through them, you can explore, question, and challenge negative belief systems that are attracting damaging connections. It enables a positive journey of self-discovery that breaks the cycle of defeating relationships and ultimately leads to a healthy outcome. Mr. Wrong gives women the courage to turn their pain into Power and their adversities into Opportunities. It also gives space for celebrating Mr. Right by acknowledging men's valuable relationship stories too. Do men get a bad rap? What role do women play in creating Mr. Wrong?

About the Author

Daniella Blechner is a South London based writer whose professional writing journey began by writing comedy sketches for Youth Project *Phenomenon '98* featuring Gina Yashere and Richard Blackwood.

She produced and wrote her first short film *Connexions*, which was Nominated for Best Screenplay at the BFM Short Film Awards in 2006 and won "Best Open Deck film" when screened at the Cutting East Festival and won the 2007 Film Fund Award from Lewisham Film Initiative to complete her poetry based short drama *Hair We Are* for the Black History Month Short Film Challenge. *Hair We Are* won the 3rd Best Film at the Images of Black Women Film Festival and has been screened at Chicago International Children's Film Festival, Pan African Film Festival, LA and BAMKids Film Festival in New York and was also screened on The Community Channel and www.itvlocal.com. Shortly afterwards, Daniella was shortlisted as a writer for Channel 4's Coming Up initiative having written a short film idea about love, marriage and dysfunctional families.

After a decade of dating disasters, Daniella chose to claim her story to empower others and wrote her debut book Mr Wrong, "a humorous and insightful exploration into why some women continually attract Mr Wrong and how to set out on a path to Mr Right."

LINKS TO STOCKISTS, RETAILERS AND SUPPLIERS

We love to add value at **Conscious Dreams Publishing** and to save you time and effort searching around, I have included several links you can click on to submit your book for consideration. Please note that these are for the mainstream, large wholesalers and headquarters of bookstores such as Waterstones. If your book is rejected, there is absolutely nothing to stop you approaching branches of these individually. In fact, the personal approach may work better than blanket emails and submissions!

Good luck! ☺

Useful Websites

Waterstones Head Office: read carefully for full details

https://www.waterstones.com/help/independent-publishers/48

Gardners Book Suppliers

http://www.gardners.com/gardners/include.aspx?l=/gardners/content/company/Selling_to_Us/gettingProductsStocked.html

Foyles

http://www.foyles.co.uk/contact-us

Your Book, Your Journey

It is now time for me, your very own Book Journey Mentor™, to leave you and, in doing so, I know that you are equipped with all the knowledge, tools and wisdom you need to prepare, plan and implement a fantastic life for your book. Remember to uphold your values, honour your noble intention or *raison d'être* and position yourself with all that is in alignment with and adds value to your book

Publishing a book is a great feeling and a great accomplishment. However planning and nurturing the life of that book by focusing on how it can create significance is creating a legacy...

Good luck with your journey and remember, it is... **Your Book, Your Journey**.

Daniella Blechner ☺

ABOUT THE AUTHOR

Daniella Blechner is a UK-based award-winning entrepreneur, founder of Conscious Dreams Publishing, bestselling author and Book Journey Mentor™ who lives in South London. She is an avid author who is passionate about transforming diverse writers into successful published authors.

Over the last five years, she has published over 170 books **and** mentored over 200 authors and aspiring authors assisting them in transforming their powerful stories and messages into successful books.

Achievements include securing international press coverage for one of her young authors, Tiana, (7) author of *My Afro* on BBC, ITV, Channel 5, Good Morning America, Breakfast Television Canada and The Kelly Clarkson Show.

Other achievements include surviving lockdown alone, gaining 400+ comments on a post about what to do with cabbage during lockdown, completing the Don't Rush Challenge, living in Tanzania as a voluntary teacher whilst getting away with speaking broken Swahili and climbing to the top of Mt Kilimanjaro! She is the author of eight books and her debut book *Mr Wrong* became a bestseller beating Steve Harvey's *Think Like a Man, Act Like a Lady*.

Daniella won the 2007 Film Fund Award from Lewisham Film Initiative to complete her poetry based short drama *Hair We Are* for the Black History Month Short Film Challenge. The film won 3rd Best Film at the Images of Black Women Film Festival and has been screened at Chicago International Children's Film Festival, Pan African Film Festival, LA and BAMKids Film Festival in New York and was also screened on ITV Local. She was also shortlisted as a writer for Channel 4's Coming Up Initiative.

Daniella is also an English teacher with 15 years' teaching experience and has published authors from 7 years old to 84. She is looking for compelling stories and page-turning plots with unique and diverse characters as well nonfiction books with powerful messages. She is passionate about providing a platform for authors to have their voices heard and stories shared so that they can educate, inspire and empower for generations to come.

- www.consciousdreamspublishing.com
- www.consciousdreamsbookshop.com
- daniella@consciousdreamspublishing.com
- www.facebook.com/consciousdreamspublishing
- www.instagram.com/consciousdreamspublishing
- www.linkedin.com/in/daniellablechner

Acknowledgements and Thank Yous

Thank you to my typesetters Nadia Vitushynska and Oksana Kosovan who never fail to be consistent, efficient and professional.

Thank you to Jae Thompson AKA CVA Jae for the phenomenal cover design. Jae never disappoints and always works with the swiftness of a hawk. Professional and creative are his middle names!

Thank you to my editors Wendy Yorke and Anna Yorke.

Thank you to my entire Conscious Dreams team, who, without you, what I do would not be possible.

Last, but not least, thank you to you. Thank you for trusting in **Conscious Dreams Publishing** and in me as your Book Journey Mentor™. Publishing a book is a big step in anyone's life and I thank you for showing up and stepping up and investing in YOU!

Conscious Dreams
PUBLISHING

Transforming diverse writers
into successful published authors

 www.consciousdreamspublishing.com

 authors@consciousdreamspublishing.com

Let's connect

www.ingramcontent.com/pod-product-compliance
Lightning Source LLC
Chambersburg PA
CBHW050718090526
44588CB00014B/2330